Christmas Dessert Recipes from Around the World

Sweets to make your holiday merry and bright

Natalie Oliver

Contents

Welcome!

Hi and Merry Christmas!

I've been so fortunate in my life to have had the opportunity to live all over the world. I'm an Army Brat and I married a Navy guy.

When I was growing up, my parents made sure we learned the culture of where we were living and we also traveled as much as my parents had time for. My mom loved to cook so she tried all the native recipes for where we were. Some were great and some weren't so great, but it was all a wonderful food adventure. Many of the recipes I still cook today are those collected from my mom that she perfected while we were stationed around the world.

Now that I have my own family and we're making the same decisions about moving from country to country that my parents made, I've got more opportunities to learn about other cultures. Spending the holidays away from the US might be sad or even daunting to some. For me, it's how I grew up so I'm very comfortable creating a Merry Christmas atmosphere where ever we happen to be. Much of the way I do that is with food.

Christmas is a wondrous time of year no matter where you celebrate it. Christmas cheer comes from within – but it's always amazing when you can share it with others around you. Creating interesting and different dishes is a wonderful way to do just that.

I hope you enjoy some of these delectable desserts and learn a little about the culture of where they're served. Bring a little international flare into your Christmas celebration!

Put some carols on and create these international sweets that will make your holidays merry and bright!

France

Buche de Noel (Yule Log)

Ingredients

4 eggs (room temperature)

2/3 cup sugar

1 teaspoon vanilla extract

1/4 teaspoon salt

1 cup cake flour

7 egg whites

1 1/3 cups granulated sugar

6 ounces unsweetened chocolate, melted and cooled

1/2 teaspoon instant espresso powder

1/2 teaspoon vanilla extract

3 cups plus 3 tablespoons butter, softened

Directions

Preheat the oven to 400°. Prepare a 10 X 15 X 1 baking sheet by buttering the bottom and sides. This size sheet is called a jelly roll sheet. Line the pan with parchment paper. Butter the parchment.

Beat the 4 whole eggs for 5 minutes. The eggs will become foamy and thick. Add the 2/3 cup of sugar, 1 tsp of vanilla extract, and salt to the eggs. Beat for 2 minutes longer.

Using a spatula, fold in the flour just two tablespoons at a time. When the flour is completely combined with the egg mixture, stop mixing to keep from over-mixing. Over-mixing will create a tough texture.

Spread the cake batter gently into the prepared jelly roll pan. Smooth the batter as much as possible without mashing it down. Bake for 10 minutes, until the cake is just set.

Turn the baked cake onto a clean, dry kitchen towel. Take the paper off and discard it. Wait about 3 minutes then roll the cake as gently as possible, in the towel. Start rolling it up at the 10 inch end.

Allow it to cool completely in the towel.

Begin the chocolate buttercream by beating the egg whites. Make sure the large mixing bowl is completely dry before placing the egg whites in it. Beat the whites on high speed until they form soft peaks. Set aside.

Combine the 1 1/3 cup of sugar and 2/3 cup water in a medium saucepan and bring it to a boil. Boil until it reduces into a slightly thickened syrup.

Go back to the egg whites and beat them on high speed. Pour the hot syrup very slowly into the whites in a steady stream.

Add in the melted chocolate, espresso powder, and vanilla extract into the egg white mixture. Continue to beat until the meringue cools completely. This will take about 5 minutes.

Continue to beat the meringue at high speed while adding the softened butter 2 tablespoons at a time. Add the butter until it's all incorporated into the frosting.

Hint: If the buttercream mixture gets loose or runny during this beating process, stop and refrigerate it. Allow it to chill completely then continue beating the butter into the meringue.

The next step is to assemble the Buche de Noel.

Unroll the cake, remove the towel, and set it aside. Evenly spread about 2 cups of the buttercream on the inside of the recently unrolled sponge cake. Because it was cooled while it was rolled in the towel, it will have a natural curve. Roll the cake following that curve with the buttercream on the inside. Gently form the cake into a roll.

Once the cake is rolled, place the seam side down and cut off the ends on each side in a diagonal. Reattach the cut off ends to the rolled cake with some of the buttercream to create branches coming off the main log.

Cover the outside of the Buche de Noel with more chocolate buttercream. Make sure you use enough buttercream to pull a knife through to simulate tree bark. Add meringue mushrooms, greenery, berries, or other decorations to complete the festive look if desired.

Chill before serving.

Dark Chocolate Espresso Tort

Ingredients

5 oz. semisweet chocolate, chopped

3 oz. unsweetened chocolate, chopped

1/4 lb. (8 Tbs.) unsalted butter, cut into pieces; more for the pan

4 eggs, at room temperature

1/2 cup sugar

1/4 cup brewed espresso or double-strength coffee, cooled to room temperature

1 Tbs. sifted, finely ground espresso beans (from about 1 heaping Tbs. whole beans)

1/4 tsp. salt

1/4 cup all-purpose flour; more for the pan

1 cup heavy whipping cream

2 tsp pure vanilla extract

2 tbsp powdered sugar (more or less, to taste)

Directions

Preheat oven to 350°. Take an 8-inch cake pan, butter the bottom and sides, then line the bottom with parchment paper. Butter the parchment and flour the pan. Shake out excess flour.

Melt the chocolates and butter together in a small, heavy saucepan. Stir frequently. Set aside.

Whip eggs, sugar, brewed espresso, ground espresso beans, and salt with the whisk attachment of an electric mixer. Use medium-high speed until the mixture is thick. This should take at least 8 minutes.

Mix in the butter and chocolate mixture on a low speed with the mixer.

Sift the flour over the top of the batter. Fold in with a spatula until all the ingredients are mixed well and incorporated.

Pour batter into the cake pan that has been prepared. Bake 25 to 30 minutes. Test by inserting a wooden toothpick into the center. If it comes back clean, the tart is done.

Cool for 15 minutes in the pan. For best results, place pan on a rack to cool.

Place the serving plate over the pan. Invert the torte easily onto the plate.   Take the paper from the bottom and discard.

Place the cream in a bowl with the vanilla and powdered sugar. Whip with the whisk attachment of an electric mixer until thick and creamy.

Slice the torte and serve with the cream.

Ginger Pear Galette

<u>Ingredients</u>

1 sheet frozen puff pastry

1 slightly beaten egg white

2 tbsp all-purpose flour

2 tbsp granulated sugar

2 tbsp brown sugar

2 tbsp finely chopped crystallized ginger

1 tsp finely shredded lemon peel

2 tbsp butter

3 large pears, halved, cored, peeled, and thinly sliced

Whipped cream for serving

<u>Directions</u>

Preheat oven to 400°.

Read and follow directions on package of frozen puff pastry for thawing. Roll out thawed puff pastry to about a 14x11-inch rectangle on a lightly floured solid surface. Trim the rolled out pastry to a 12x10-inch rectangle.

Line a baking sheet with parchment paper. Place the trimmed pastry on the prepared baking sheet. Using a fork, prick pastry evenly over the surface.

Create an edge by folding about 1/2 inch of pastry back over itself all the way around it. Brush around the edges with the beaten egg white. Decorate edges with small cutouts or designs from pastry trimmings or simply crimp them. Brush one more time with beaten egg whites.

Place flour, granulated sugar, brown sugar, 1 tablespoon crystallized ginger, and lemon peel into a small mixing bowl. Stir together. Cut butter into the dry mixture until pieces are pea sized.

Sprinkle about half of the butter and ginger mixture over the waiting pastry. Evenly arrange the pear slices on top next. Overlap the slices slightly. When pears are arranged, sprinkle the rest of the butter and ginger mixture over them.

Bake, uncovered, for 18 to 20 minutes. Pastry will be golden brown and pears will be tender.

Serve warm with whipped cream and a sprinkle of the remaining crystallized ginger.

England

Sherry Trifle

Ingredients

4 1/2 oz butter (room temperature)

1/2 cup sugar

2 large eggs

5 oz self-rising flour

6 tablespoons seedless raspberry jam

8 tablespoons sweet sherry

12 ounces fresh raspberries

1 pint milk

1 vanilla pod

4 egg yolks

1 tbsp sugar

1 1/2 tbsp cornstarch

3/4 pint whipping cream

2 oz sliced almonds, toasted

Fresh raspberries

Silver sugar nonpareils

Directions

Preheat oven to 350°.

Place the butter, sugar, and eggs into a medium mixing bowl. Beat until mixed. Add the flour and continue to beat until smooth. Do not over-beat.

Pour batter into a 10" cake pan. Tap lightly on the counter top to release any air bubbles. Bake for 20-30 minutes until lightly browned.

Cool completely on a wire rack.

Place the raspberries in a small bowl and toss with half of the sherry. Set aside and let macerate.

Cut the cooled cake into 2" squares and slice in half horizontally. Liberally spread raspberry jam on each bottom layer and place the top back on.

Place each raspberry cake sandwich in the bottom of a glass trifle bowl. Sprinkle with the other half of the sherry. Set aside.

To make the custard, pour the milk into a small, heavy saucepan. Turn the heat to medium. Split the vanilla pod down the center and scrape the seeds from the insides of the pod. Add the seeds and the pod to the milk. Slowly bring the milk and vanilla to almost boiling.

Place a large glass bowl in the freezer to chill it for the finished custard.

Remove from heat and pour milk into a bowl to infuse. Set aside for about 10 minutes.

After 10 minutes or so, remove the vanilla pod from the milk and discard it.

Place the egg yolks in a large mixing bowl and whisk them gently. Add the cornstarch and sugar and continue to whisk. Add the cooled milk and continue to whisk.

Rinse the saucepan used for the milk for reuse. Strain the liquid through a fine sieve back into the rinsed saucepan.

Gently cook the custard mixture over medium low heat , stirring constantly. The custard will start to thicken. Do not allow this mixture to boil.

Gather a very large bowl and fill it half way with ice. Set aside.

Continue cooking for 2 minutes longer. The custard will be a very thick pouring consistency. Take the glass bowl from the freezer and quickly pour the custard into it. Place the bowl of custard in the large bowl of ice and continue to whisk to cool custard. When custard has cooled considerably, place a sheet of plastic wrap directly on top of the custard to prevent a skin from forming and set it aside still sitting in the ice bowl.

Gently whip the cream until it nearly holds its shape, then spoon three quarters of it on top of the custard and carefully spread to the sides of the bowl.

Whip the remaining whipping cream until it's thick enough to spread.

To finish assembling the trifle, add the macerated raspberries and juice to the trifle bowl on top of the sponge cake sandwiches. Spoon the chilled custard onto the raspberries. Spread the whipped cream as the next layer to the trifle. Smooth the cream out. Decorate the top with the toasted almond slices, fresh raspberries, and the silver sugar nonpareils.

Cover with plastic wrap and chill until ready to serve.

Date and Apricot Packets

<u>Ingredients</u>

6 sheets filo pastry, about 6¼ oz in total

1½ oz unsalted butter, melted

1 tbsp powdered sugar

4 oz dried apricots, finely chopped

4 oz dried dates, finely chopped

4 tbsp fresh orange juice

Finely grated orange zest from one orange

½ tsp ground cinnamon

1 oz chopped pistachios

<u>Directions</u>

Preheat oven to 400°. Place the dried fruit in a bowl with the orange juice. Mix well. Let stand for one hour for the juice to be absorbed into the fruit.

Add orange zest, pistachios, and cinnamon. Mix well.

Lay filo dough sheets out on a flat surface. Stack each layer and then cut into six equal squares, about six inches each. Trim and discard any excess.

Brush each filo square with the melted butter. Start each packet by offsetting the corners of three squares. Make twelve packets with three filo squares each.

Place one tablespoon of the fruit and juice mixture on each packet. When mixture is evenly distributed, gather the edges and pinch at the top to create a little packet.

Line a baking sheet with parchment paper and spray lightly with cooking spray. Place each pastry packet on the parchment. Use the remaining butter and lightly brush each pastry.

Bake until golden brown, approximately 12-15 minutes. Dust with powdered sugar and serve.

Japan

Japanese Strawberry Shortcake

Ingredients

4 large eggs, white and yolks separated

4.2 ounces (9.5 tablespoons) granulated sugar, sifted

3 tablespoons milk, at room temperature

1/2 teaspoon pure vanilla extract

4.2 ounces (14 tablespoons) cake flour, sifted

1.2 ounces (2.3 tablespoons) butter, melted

———

1 teaspoon unflavored gelatin

4 teaspoons cold water

1 cup cold heavy whipping cream

1/4 cup powdered sugar

1/2 teaspoon vanilla extract

1/4 cup granulated sugar

1/4 cup water

10 ounces fresh strawberries

Preheat the oven to 350°. Take an 8-inch cake pan, butter the bottom and sides, then line the bottom with parchment paper. Butter the parchment and flour the pan. Shake out excess flour.

Add the 9.5 tablespoons of sugar to the egg whites in a large mixing bowl. Beat the whites until stiff.

When whites are stiffly beaten, add the yolks to the mixture. Whisk gently until the yolks are incorporated.

First add the milk to the egg and sugar mixture. Next add the pure vanilla extract to the mixture. Finally add the flour to the mixture. Fold everything together gently with a spatula.

Add the melted butter and continue to fold all ingredients together.

Place the batter for the cake into the round cake pan that you prepared. Gently tap the pan on the counter top to remove air bubbles in the batter.

Bake for 25 to 30 minutes. Check the cake for doneness by lightly pressing the top. If it springs back, the cake is done. The cake will be golden brown.

Cool the cake completely before handling on a wire rack. Loosen the cake from the pan by running a knife around the inside of the pan. Remove the cake to a plate.

Start the whipped cream frosting by placing the cold water in a small saucepan. Sprinkle the gelatin into the water. Do not stir. Let this stand for 5 minutes.

After the standing time, stir the gelatin and water and put over low heat. Continue to stir until the gelatin is completely dissolved. Take the saucepan from the heat. Set aside to cool to room temperature.

Combine the whipping cream, 1/4 cup of powdered sugar, and vanilla in a mixing bowl. Beat just until thickened slightly. Slowly pour the cooled gelatin mixture while mixing on low speed into the whipped cream mixture. Once ingredients are incorporated together, whip at high speed until stiff.

Combine the 1/4 cup of granulated sugar and the 1/4 cup of water. Bring to a boil and stir until all the sugar is completely dissolved. Boil for 30 seconds more. Set aside to cool to room temperature.

Begin assembling the cake when all components are complete and cooled. Wash and hull strawberries. Save 10 strawberries for decorating the top of the cake. Slice the remaining berries into slices and set aside.

Carefully slice the cake horizontally into 2 layers using a long serrated knife.

Place one layer cut-side up on the serving plate. Brush the cut surface of the cake with the cooled simple syrup. Be careful of the amount you use – too much will make the cake soggy and too little will make the cake drier.

After applying the syrup, add a thin layer of whipped cream. Smooth it completely over the top of the layer. Arrange fresh strawberry slices on top of the whipped cream.

Add a second layer of whipped cream on top of the fresh berries.

Brush more of the syrup onto the cut side of the second layer of cake. Place this layer cut side down on top of the first layer and the cream.

Continue to add whipped cream and frost the sides and top. Use the rest of the cream to finish frosting the cake. Decorate the top of the cake with the reserved strawberries.

Sweden

St Lucia Saffron Rolls

Ingredients

2 cups milk

1 1/4 oz package active dry yeast

1/2 cup sugar

2 tbsp brandy

1 tsp powdered saffron

4-5 cups unbleached all-purpose flour, or more as needed

1/2-1 tsp ground cardamom

1/2 tsp salt

1/4 cup dark raisins

1 large egg, lightly beaten with 1 tbsp water for egg wash

Directions

Add milk to a small saucepan and heat until warm. Remove from heat.

Combine yeast, pinch of sugar, and 1/4 cup of the warmed milk in a small mixing bowl.   Let this yeast mixture stand for 10 minutes. The mixture will become bubbly.

Combine 2 tablespoons of the milk, brandy, 1 teaspoon of the sugar, and the saffron in another small mixing bowl. Stir well until the sugar is dissolved. Hold the remaining milk until later.

Whisk together 4 cups of the flour, the remaining sugar, the cardamom, and salt into a large mixing bowl. Make a well in the center of the dry ingredients. Pour in the wet ingredients including the yeast mixture, the saffron mixture, and the remaining milk.

Use an electric mixer or stir with a wooden spoon to combine all ingredients. Gradually add extra flour as needed to form a soft dough.

Place the dough on a lightly floured surface. Knead for 10 to 15 minutes, until the dough is elastic and smooth. Add flour as necessary during the kneading process. Knead the raisins into the dough.

Roll dough into a ball. Place the dough into a large, lightly oiled bowl. Turn the dough inside the bowl to coat with the oil. Cover with a damp towel. Place in a warm spot and let it rise until doubled, about 30 minutes.

Punch the dough down. Transfer to a lightly floured surface. Roll the dough into a long log. Cut into 12 equal smaller rolled pieces.

Roll each piece until it's 8 inches long. Twist to form a figure eight. Decorate with a raisin in the center of each end.

Prepare a baking sheet by lining it with parchment. Place each roll about 2 inches apart on the sheet. Cover with a damp towel to rise for a final time. Let stand for about 30 minutes, or until almost doubled in size.

Preheat the oven to 375°.

When oven is ready, bake the rolls for 30 minutes. When done, the bottom of a roll will sound hollow when tapped. Lightly brush the roll tops with the egg wash.

Germany

Gingerbread

<u>Ingredients</u>

1 cup butter, softened

2 cups packed brown sugar

3 eggs

2/3 cup honey

1/4 cup orange liqueur

1 cup sour cream

1/2 cup orange juice

1 2/3 cups all-purpose flour

1 cup whole wheat flour

4 teaspoons baking powder

2 teaspoons ground ginger

1 teaspoon ground cinnamon

1/4 teaspoon ground nutmeg

1/4 teaspoon ground cloves

1 cup raisins

1 cup blanched slivered almonds

Powdered sugar for dusting

Directions

Preheat the oven to 350°.

Place the flours, baking powder, ginger, cinnamon, nutmeg, and cloves into a large mixing bowl. Whisk together well.

Cream the butter together with the brown sugar in another large mixing bowl. Slowly beat the eggs into the mixture. Add the honey, liqueur, sour cream, and juice one by one. Mix well.

Gently beat the flour mixture into the creamed mixture in stages. Stir in the raisins and almonds when the mixture is well mixed.

Pour the batter into a greased and floured tube pan or into two small loaf pans.

Bake in the preheated oven for 80 minutes. The gingerbread will be done when a toothpick inserted into the middle comes back clean. Cool on a rack. Dust generously with powdered sugar.

South Africa

Christmas Pudding Ice Cream

<u>Ingredients</u>

4 large eggs

2/3 cup super-fine sugar

1 1/4 cup heavy whipping cream

1/2 cup dried fruit and nuts

3 tbsp brandy

1 tsp cinnamon

1/2 tsp ginger

1/2 tsp nutmeg

<u>Directions</u>

Add two tablespoons of brandy to the dried fruit and nuts. Let stand at least for four hours or overnight.

Separate the eggs, reserving the whites in a separate bowl. Place the yolks in a medium mixing bowl. Beat together with the sugar until the mixture is thickened and creamy.

To the egg mixture, add the cinnamon, ginger, nutmeg, and the remaining brandy.   Set aside.

Place the heavy cream in a large mixing bowl. Whip the cream until firm. Set aside.

Beat the egg whites until they form peaks. Set aside.

Take the whipped cream and stir it into the yolks and sugar mixture. Add half of the fruit mixture.

Fold the egg whites into the whipped cream mixture gently using a spatula. Add the rest of the fruit mixture.

Pour into a lightly buttered plastic bowl with a smooth rounded bottom. Cover and freeze overnight.

When ready to serve, remove the bowl of ice cream from the freezer and dip in hot water. Turn the molded ice cream out onto a serving platter. Serve immediately. Garnish with fresh berries if desired.

Brazil

Rabanadas

<u>Ingredients</u>

1 day old baguette

2 cups milk

4 eggs

Butter for frying

Sugar for dusting

Cinnamon powder

4 cups water

1 cup dry port wine

1 stick cinnamon, about 2 inches long

2/3 cup honey

Directions

Slice the baguette into 1 inch slices.

Make the port wine sauce. Combine the water, wine, cinnamon stick, and honey in a large heavy saucepan. Bring slowly to a boil while stirring over medium heat. When it begins to boil, reduce the heat but do not stop the boil.

Continue to cook slowly at a very low boil for 10 minutes. Remove the cinnamon stick. The syrup will be thickened and reduced by one half. Remove from heat and cool to room temperature.

In a shallow bowl, blend the eggs and milk. Dip the bread into the egg mixture and make sure all surfaces of the bread are covered. Let the bread sit in the egg mixture for several minutes to soak it up.

Heat a large frying pan on medium heat. Add butter to the pan to melt.

Place saturated bread slices into the warm melted butter in frying pan. Cook on both sides until they are golden brown. Adjust the heat as necessary through the cooking process to not burn them and ensure they are warmed through.

Dust each slice in sugar taking care to make sure that each piece is liberally coated. Sprinkle with cinnamon powder.

Serve with the port wine sauce drizzled on top or served on the side.

Australia

Mulled Fruit with Spiced Custard

Ingredients

1 bottle of red wine

1/2 cup super-fine sugar

2 fresh bay leaves

12 cloves

3 star anise

2 cinnamon quills

1 cup maraschino cherries

2 tsp arrowroot

1 1/2 cups chopped fresh pineapple

1 cup strawberries, hulled, halved

2 oranges, peeled, sliced

———————

3 cups whole milk

2 fresh bay leaves

2 cardamom pods

1 vanilla bean, split, seeds scraped

5 egg yolks

1/2 cup super-fine sugar

1 1/2 tbs cornstarch

Directions

Combine the wine, sugar, bay leaves, and spices in a medium saucepan. Heat over low heat and stir until sugar is dissolved. Raise heat to simmer the mixture. Continue to simmer for 15 more minutes.

Dissolve the arrowroot in a small amount of cold water. Ladle a little of the hot wine mixture into the arrowroot and water. Pour back into the saucepan with the rest of the wine mixture and cook until it is slightly reduced, about another 5-7 minutes. Cool.

Place all the fruit in a mixing bowl. Pour the wine mixture over the fruit. Cover and refrigerate for at least 2 hours.

Make the custard by taking the whole milk, bay leaves, cardamom, and vanilla and placing them in a medium saucepan. Heat the mixture over medium heat.

Bring it to boiling point, then take it off the heat. Set it aside for 15 minutes to infuse.

Whisk together the egg yolks, sugar and cornstarch. Strain the infused milk mixture and add it to the yolks and sugar mixture.

Return the saucepan to the heat and stir over low heat for 5 minutes. Mixture will thicken. Serve with mulled fruits.

Antarctica

Apricot-Almond Ice Cream Layered Dessert

Ingredients

1 package (12 ounces) vanilla wafers, crushed

1 1/3 cups chopped almonds, toasted

1/2 cup butter, melted

1 tbsp almond extract

6 cups vanilla ice cream, softened

1 jar (18 ounces) apricot preserves

Directions

Combine the cookie crumbs and almonds in a large mixing bowl. Add the melted butter butter and almond extract. Mix well until crumbs are slightly moistened.

Pat a third of the crumb mixture into an ungreased glass 13 X 9 container. Freeze for 15 minutes.

Spread half of the softened ice cream gently over the frozen crust. Be careful not to loosen the crust and have it mix with the ice cream.

Gently spoon half of the apricot preserves over the ice cream layer of the dessert.

Sprinkle the preserves layer with half of the crumb mixture that remains. Freeze for about 30 minutes.

Repeat layers until components are gone. Freeze. Cut into squares to serve. Garnish with toasted almonds and whipped cream if desired.

China

Five Spice Chocolate Cake

Ingredients

7 oz unsweetened chocolate, finely chopped

6 oz bittersweet chocolate, finely chopped

1/2 cup water

1 1/4 cups sugar

4 tsp Chinese five-spice powder

2 1/4 sticks unsalted butter, cut into pieces and softened

6 large eggs

2 cups chilled heavy whipping cream

1/4 cup finely chopped crystallized ginger

Description

Preheat oven to 350°. Prepare a 10 inch round cake pan by buttering the bottom and sides. Use parchment paper to line the bottom of the pan. Butter the exposed paper on the bottom.

Place both chocolates in a large shallow bowl. Set aside.

Bring the water, 1/2 cup of the sugar, and the five spice to a boil. Stir well until the sugar dissolves. Pour the hot liquid through a fine sieve over the chocolates in the dish. Stir until the chocolate is melted and smooth. Stir in the butter until melted and smooth.

In a separate mixing bowl, beat the eggs with the remaining sugar until they become pale and the volume increases. Beaters will leave a trail as they mix when the mixture is ready. This can take up to 20 minutes with a hand held mixer or 10 minutes with a stand up mixer.

Stir 1/4 of the egg mixture into the chocolate mixture to lighten it. Then gently fold in the remainder thoroughly. This folding will take 1 to 2 minutes for mixture to be fully blended.

Pour batter into the prepared pan and smooth the top. Place the pan of batter in a water bath with water halfway up the side of the pan. Bake in the middle of the oven for 40 to 45 minutes. Cake will be done when a toothpick tester inserted in center comes out with moist crumbs adhering. Remove from water bath and the oven. Cool at least 2 hours in pan on a rack.

To unmold the cake, run a blade around the edge of the pan and briefly heat the cake pan on the stove top for about 10 seconds on medium heat. Place serving plate over the pan and turn cake onto the plate. Remove paper and discard.

To make the ginger cream, beat the heavy cream to form soft peaks. Using a spatula, fold in the crystallized ginger.

Serve the cake at room temperature with the chilled cream.

Thailand

Thai Style Crème Caramel

<u>Ingredients</u>

1 cup coconut milk – not reduced or fat free

2 eggs

1 tbsp sugar

1/4 tsp pandan essence/paste (available in tiny bottles at Asian/Chinese food stores), OR 1 tsp vanilla plus two drops of green food coloring

1/4 cup (or more) maple syrup

Pinch of salt

Coconut oil or canola oil

<u>Directions</u>

Preheat oven to 350°. Lightly grease four oven-proof ramekins with oil.

Beat the eggs with a whisk or with an electric mixer for about 1 minute. Add the salt, sugar, pandan paste (or vanilla and green food coloring), and the coconut milk. Stir well until completely combined.

Pour enough maple syrup into the bottom of each ramekin to completely cover the bottom. This will be around a tablespoon or maybe a little more depending on the ramekin.

Pour the custard into each ramekin and fill to about 3/4 full. Syrup will remain at the bottom and this is what you want. Do not stir.

Place the ramekins in a large and deep dish or pan. Fill with water until it reaches about one quarter of the way up the side of the ramekins.

Bake for 30 minutes, or until a knife inserted into the center comes back clean. Cool completely. Refrigerate until ready to serve.

To serve, loosen custard by running a knife around the inner rim of each ramekin. Turn each ramekin over onto an individual serving plate. The pudding will come out easily, and the syrup will drip down the side of each custard.

Vietnam

Banana Rice Pudding

<u>Ingredients</u>

1 1/2 cups brown rice (cooked)

1 cup nonfat milk

1 banana (medium, sliced)

15 oz lychees, sliced (pears or grapes are good substitutes)

1/4 cup water

2 tbsp honey

1 tsp pure vanilla extract

1/2 tsp ground cinnamon

1/2 tsp ground nutmeg

Directions

Drain lychees or other fruit if not using lychees.

Combine the lychee slices and the banana slices in a medium saucepan. Add the water, honey, vanilla, cinnamon, and nutmeg.

Bring the mixture to a boil. Immediately reduce the heat and gently simmer for about 10 minutes. The fruit should be tender, but not mushy.

Once the fruit is tender, add the milk and stir. Then add the rice and mix thoroughly.

Bring the mixture to a boil again and reduce to a simmer. Continue the simmer for 10 more minutes.

Serve warm or cold.

Italy

Struffoli

Ingredients

2 2/3 cup all-purpose flour

4 eggs

1 egg yolk

Scant 1/4 cup sugar

2.5 oz butter

6 oz Limoncello

Grated peel from half a lemon

Salt

Vegetable oil for frying

1 1/2 cups honey

Colored candy sprinkles

1/2 cup candied orange

Directions

Take all the flour and mound it up on a hard surface countertop. In a medium mixing bowl, combine the whole eggs, the egg yolk, butter, sugar, lemon peel, Limoncello, and a dash of salt. Make a well in the middle of the flour and gradually add the combined wet ingredients from the mixing bowl.

Start blending together slowly to begin incorporating the wet ingredients with the flour. Continue to blend and then knead until smooth. A well formed dough will result. Shape into a ball, cover it with plastic wrap, and set it aside for half an hour.

After 30 minutes, lightly knead the dough again briefly. Divide it into balls about the size of medium oranges. Roll each ball into round strips about the width of your finger. Cut them into into small pieces resembling gnocchi and place them on a cloth sprinkled with flour.

Move to a sieve and gently shake just before frying to remove excess flour.

Heat the frying oil to 350°. When the oil is to temperature, fry a few pieces of dough at a time in plenty of boiling oil. When they're done they will swell and turn golden. Don't let them get too dark. Drain the cooked dough on paper towels.

Heat the honey in a fairly large saucepan. When the honey is warm and runny, take it off the heat. Add the fried dough pieces. Stir gently to soak each piece in honey. Add about half of the candy sprinkles and chopped candied orange and gently stir again.

Place the honey coated pieces of cooked dough on a serving plate. Sprinkle the remaining candied fruit and sprinkles on the top of the struffoli to decorate.

Mini Panettone

<u>Ingredients</u>

1 package active dry yeast

9 oz milk

2 2/3 cup all-purpose flour

3/4 cup sugar, softened

Salt

6 egg yolks

7 oz butter

1/3 cup raisins

1/2 cup candied citrus peel

3 tbsp Cognac

Powdered sugar for dusting

Directions

Preheat oven to 375°.

Butter 6 mini cake tins and line them with parchment paper. Butter the top of the parchment paper.

Mix the raisins, mixed peel, and the Cognac. Let stand until needed.

In a large mixing bowl, completely dissolve the yeast in the milk. When yeast is dissolved, stir in flour, sugar, and a pinch of salt. Next, add the egg yolks and the butter. Mix well. Begin kneading when the dough forms a ball. Knead well. Let the dough rise covered with a damp towel in a warm place until it has doubled in size.

Take the raisin and Cognac mixture and begin kneading it into the risen dough. Cover with a damp towel and leave to rise for another 30 minutes.

After the second rising, divide the dough into six equal pieces. Shape the six pieces into balls and place each one into the cake tins. Let to rise uncovered for around 20 minutes.

Bake on the bottom rack around 1 hour. Cakes are done when a toothpick inserted into the middle comes back clean.

Check the cakes after 35-40 minutes and cover with foil if they are browning on top too quickly. When the cakes test done, remove from the oven and cool in the tins.

When ready to serve, remove from the tins. Take the paper away and discard it. Place individual Panettones on serving plates and dust generously with powdered sugar.

United States of America

Southern Pecan Pie

Ingredients

1 cup light brown sugar, packed

1/2 cup granulated sugar

2 large eggs

1 cup chopped pecans

1/2 cup butter (1 stick), melted

2 tablespoons milk

1 tablespoon all-purpose flour

1 1/2 teaspoons vanilla extract

One 9-inch deep dish pie shell, unbaked, or homemade pastry

1 cup pecan halves

Vanilla ice cream or whipped cream, for serving

<u>Directions</u>

Preheat oven to 325°.

In a large mixing bowl, combine the sugars and the eggs. Beat together until creamy. Add the chopped pecans, melted butter, milk, flour, and vanilla extract. Stir gently to combine.

Pour the egg and sugar mixture into the pie shell. Be careful not to overfill. Arrange the pecan halves on top of the filling.

Put the pie in the center of the oven and bake for 55 minutes. To check for doneness, shake pie slightly. There should only be a small movement in the center and the pie should be mostly firm. It will set up a little more as it cools.

Serve each slice topped with vanilla ice cream or sweetened whipped cream.

Simple Sugar Cookies

Ingredients

2/3 cup butter, softened

3/4 cup sugar

1 tsp baking powder

1/4 tsp salt

1 egg

1 tbsp milk

1 tsp pure vanilla extract

2 cups all purpose flour

Directions

Place butter into a large mixing bowl. Cream butter with an electric mixer on medium high speed for 30 seconds. Add sugar, baking powder, and salt. Continue to cream together until combined.

Beat in egg, milk, and vanilla extract. Continue to mix until well combined. Start adding flour about 1/2 cup at a time. Continue to mix using the electric mixer until the dough is too thick. Use a wooden spoon to stir in the remaining flour.

Divide cookie dough in half and wrap each separately in plastic wrap. Chill for about 2 hours or more.

Preheat oven to 375°.

Lightly flour a solid surface such as a counter top. Take one portion of the dough from the refrigerator and roll it out to about 1/4 inch thick. Using 2-1/2 inch cookie cutters in Christmas shapes, cut individual cookies out. Place each cookie about 1 inch apart on an ungreased cookie sheet. Sprinkle each cookie with colored sugar. Repeat with the second portion of chilled dough. Bake for 7 to 10 minutes until edges are lightly browned. Be careful to not over-bake. Cool cookies on a wire rack.

Divinity

Ingredients

2 1/2 cups sugar

1/2 cup water

1/2 cup light corn syrup

1/4 teaspoon salt

2 egg whites

1 teaspoon vanilla extract

1 cup chopped pecans, toasted

Toasted pecan halves for garnish

Directions

Cook sugar, water, corn syrup, and salt in a heavy large saucepan over low heat until sugar dissolves. Continue cooking without stirring until a candy thermometer registers 248°. This will take about 15 minutes. Remove the syrup mixture from heat.

While the sugar mixture is cooking, beat egg whites with an electric mixer at high speed until stiff peaks form. When the sugar mixture has been taken from the heat, pour half of it over egg whites in a very thin, continuous stream. Beat constantly at high speed, while adding the syrup. This will take about 5 minutes. The process of adding the syrup while mixing is difficult with only one set of hands. If you don't have a helper, use a stand up mixer if you have one.

Cook the remaining sugar syrup over medium heat, stirring occasionally, until a candy thermometer registers 272°. This will take about 4 to 5 minutes.

Add the vanilla extract into the egg white mixture and mix. Slowly pour hot syrup in a constant and thin stream over the egg white mixture. Continue beating constantly at high speed until the mixture holds its shape. This will take about 6 to 8 minutes. Stir in the toasted, chopped pecans.

Using two spoons, drop mixture as quickly as possible onto lightly greased wax paper.   Use one spoon to push each dollop off of the other spoon. Press a toasted pecan half into each dollop of divinity before it sets up.

Cool and serve.

Poland

Rum Babka (Buttermilk Rum Cake)

Ingredients

1/2 pound (2 sticks) butter, softened

2 cups sugar

4 eggs, at room temperature

3 cups all-purpose flour

1/2 teaspoon baking soda

1 cup buttermilk, at room temperature

1 teaspoon pure vanilla extract

_____

 1 cup sugar

1 1/2 cups water

4 teaspoons lemon zest

2 tablespoons orange zest

1 teaspoon pure vanilla extract

2/3 cup dark rum

_____

2/3 cup sugar

 1/4 cup butter

 1/3 cup orange juice

<u>Directions</u>

Preheat oven to 350°.

Cream the butter and 2 cups of sugar together in a large mixing bowl until light and fluffy. Beat in the eggs one at a time. Mix well.

Combine flour and baking soda in a separate mixing bowl. Add the butter mixture and mix well. Add buttermilk and vanilla. Mix to incorporate completely. Pour batter into a 10 inch tube pan that has been greased well with butter.

Bake for 1 hour. Cake will be done when a toothpick inserted into the center comes back clean. Cool on wire rack for 20 minutes. Place a serving plate over the tube pan and turn the cake out on to the plate.

While the cake bakes, make the rum syrup. Place 1 cup of sugar, the water, and the citrus zests into a small saucepan. Stir constantly over high heat to completely dissolve sugar. This will take about 5 minutes.

When the sugar is dissolved, strain the syrup mixture into a glass mixing bowl and cool. When the liquid is cool, add the vanilla and rum. Stir well. Set aside.

While cake is still warm, but not still steaming hot, poke holes into the top surface. Slowly pour about a quarter or a third of the rum syrup over the cake. The syrup will seep into the cake through the holes you punched. When the first pour has been absorbed, pour the next round of syrup. You might have to do this a few times to use all the syrup.

As you wait for the cake to absorb the rum syrup, make the glaze. Melt the 1/4 cup of butter in a small saucepan. Add the 2/3 cup of sugar and the orange juice. Cook over medium heat to melt the sugar. Bring to a boil and boil for about one minute.

Pour the glaze over the completely cooled cake that has absorbed the rum syrup. The glaze will drip down the sides of the cake.

Spain

Pestiños (Anise Cookies)

Ingredients

3 1/2 oz olive oil

Rind of 1 lemon

4 tsp anise seeds

3 1/2 oz white wine

2 oz anise liqueur

2 cups all purpose flour

2 cups canola oil for frying

2 cups honey

1 tsp water

Directions

Cut the peel from the lemon in strips. In a 10 inch heavy frying pan, fry lemon peel slices in the olive oil until it turns brown. Take pan from heat. Add the anise seeds.

Stir and set aside so oil will cool. Remove the lemon peel and discard it.

Add the wine and liqueur to a large mixing bowl. Add the cooled olive oil with the anise seeds. Stir well. Add the flour. Mix well to incorporate all ingredients. The dough will form a ball. Cover the dough in the bowl with a damp towel and let sit in a warm spot for 30 minutes.

Generously flour a solid surface such as a counter top. Place dough on the surface and roll it out to about 1/8 inch thick. Using a pizza cutter or a sharp chef's knife, cut the dough into strips about 1-inch wide and 2-inches long.

Heat the canola oil to 350°. When the oil reaches the appropriate temperature, fry pestinos until golden brown. Drain on paper towels.

Combine the honey and water in a small sauce pan. Heat over low heat and stir well. Dip pestinos into the honey a few at a time to coat each one.

Place on serving platter.

Turrón de Navidad

Ingredients

1 3/4 cup roasted almond slivers

1 1/2 cups honey

3 egg whites

Directions

Preheat oven to 375°. Also prepare a square baking dish by lining it with parchment paper.

Roast the almonds in the oven for 10 minutes. Toss almonds after about 5 minutes.

Place the honey in medium sized saucepan. Bring it to a slow boil over medium heat. As the boil begins, take it off the heat and set it aside.

Beat egg whites to the strong peak stage. Fold the whites gently into the honey.

Once the honey and egg whites are combined, continue to stir and bring the mixture back up to medium heat. Stir constantly for 15-20 minutes. The meringue honey mixture will begin to increase in volume. Continue to stir. Eventually the mixture will condense to a thick caramel like consistency. The color will become a deeper golden brown.

Test if the mixture is ready by placing a small amount on a plate and putting it in the refrigerator for about 1 minute. If the bit on the plate hardens, the mixture is ready to stop cooking.

When you take the mixture from the heat, add the roasted almonds. Mix well. Pour the turron mixture as quickly as possible into the prepared dish. Take another piece of parchment paper and press it down directly on top of the mixture.   This will help make the bars more uniform when they are cut.

Place the pan in the refrigerator to cool. After about 3 hours, remove and cut into small bars.

Mexico

Rompope (Eggnog)

Ingredients

4 cups milk

3⁄4 cup sugar

1 cinnamon stick

6 egg yolks

2⁄3 cup light or golden rum

1 tsp. vanilla extract

Directions

In a large and tall saucepan, combine milk, sugar, and cinnamon stick. Stir well. Bring to a boil over medium-high heat. Do not stir the milk as it heats. Skim any skin that forms on the top of the liquid with a spoon and discard it. Continue to boil and reduce the mixture until it measure about 2 3/4 cups. This should take about 25 minutes. Take the cinnamon stick out and discard.

Vigorously whisk egg yolks in a medium mixing bowl. Slowly drizzle the hot milk into the egg yolks while continuing to whisk.

Prepare a large bowl with ice water to cool mixture when finished cooking. Set aside until needed.

Place the mixing bowl over gently simmering water in a saucepan. Do not allow the bottom of the bowl to touch the simmering water. Cook the mixture and stir constantly until the mixture reaches 175°. The mixture will coat the back of the spoon. This will take about 5 minutes.

Immediately place the bowl in the prepared ice water. Stir often until cool. Whisk in the rum and vanilla.

Strain the mixture through a fine sieve into a covered storage container. Chill in the refrigerator for at least 8 hours. Serve chilled.

Cabalerros Ricos (Bread Pudding Souffle with Almonds and Cinnamon Syrup)

Ingredients

2 cups whole milk

1 1/4 cup granulated sugar

16 1/2-inch slices French bread

4 egg whites

2 egg yolks

Vegetable oil for shallow-fat frying

1 cup water

1 cup packed brown sugar

2 whole cloves

4 4-inch sticks cinnamon

1/2 cup almonds, coarsely chopped

1/4 cup coffee flavored liqueur or strong brewed coffee

Ice cream for serving

Directions

Preheat oven to 350°.

Combine milk and the 1/4 cup of the granulated sugar in a fairly shallow dish. Stir to dissolve sugar. Place the bread slices into the milk mixture and allow to soak for about 2-3 minutes. Take them out and place them in a colander to drain.

In a large mixing bowl beat the egg whites with an electric mixer to the stiff peak stage. In a small mixing bowl beat the egg yolks with an electric mixer until they turn a lemon color. This should take about 3-5 minutes. Fold the beaten egg yolks into the egg whites gently with a spatula.

Add about a half inch of vegetable oil into a heavy 12-inch frying pan. Heat the oil over medium-high heat until a drop of water will sizzle. Reduce heat slightly. Dip the reserved milk soaked bread slices into the egg mixture one piece at a time. Make sure each slice of bread is completely coated in the egg mixture. Fry the bread in the hot oil turning once until golden brown on both sides. Do not get the oil too hot or the bread will burn. Do not crowd the pan with bread slices or the oil will get too cool. Drain on paper towels.

To make the syrup, combine the water, 1 cup of the granulated sugar, the brown sugar, and cloves in a saucepan. Slowly bring mixture to a simmer over medium heat. Stir often to help dissolve sugar. Add the cinnamon stick.

Continue to cook for about 8 minutes. Mixture will thicken to about the consistency of maple syrup. Strain the syrup through a fine-mesh sieve or several layers of cheesecloth. Discard anything left in the sieve.

Return the strained syrup to the saucepan. Add the almonds and the liqueur. Bring to a boil on high heat. Reduce heat to simmer and cook uncovered the mixture reduces to about 1-1/2 cups. This should take about 4 minutes.

Place half of the fried bread slices in a single layer in a rectangular baking dish. Pour half of the syrup over the bread slices making sure that each slice gets some syrup. Repeat the layers.

Place in the hot oven and bake, uncovered, until syrup is bubbly and the top is browned slightly. This should take about 25-30 minutes.

Serve warm with ice cream.

Greece

Pistachio Baklava Cups

Ingredients

2 packages (1.9 oz each) mini–fillo shells

1 cup honey

2 tsp lemon juice

1 cup shelled pistachios

3 tbsp sugar

1/2 tsp ground cinnamon

1/4 tsp ground cloves

1 tbsp melted butter

Directions

Preheat oven to 350°.

Lay fillo shells out on a rimmed baking sheet. Combine honey and lemon juice in small mixing bowl. Mix well. Set aside.

Chop pistachios. Use a food processor if desired but be careful to chop and not mince nuts. Combine chopped nuts, sugar, cinnamon, cloves, and melted butter in a mixing bowl. Mix well.

Using a table spoon, place a spoonful into each shell. Place into the hot oven and bake 8 to 10 minutes. Edges of shells will be lightly browned.

Warm the honey and lemon juice mixture slightly to make it easier to pour. Pour about a teaspoon of the warmed honey mixture over the warm Bakalava cups. Cool the cups on the backing sheet.

Melomacarona   (Honey-Dipped Cookies)

<u>Ingredients</u>

1 3/4 cups mild-flavored olive oil

1 3/4 cups sugar

1 tbsp orange zest

1/2 cup orange juice

2 tbsp cognac

2 1/2 tsp ground cinnamon

1 1/2 tsp baking soda

3/4 teaspoon freshly grated nutmeg

1/4 tsp salt

1/4 tsp ground cloves

7 cups all-purpose flour

1 egg white, lightly beaten

1/2 cup finely chopped almonds

1 recipe Spiced Honey Glaze (recipe below)

Directions

Preheat oven to 350°.

Whisk olive oil, 1-1/4 cups of the sugar, the orange zest, orange juice, cognac, 2 teaspoons of the cinnamon, the baking soda, nutmeg, salt, and cloves in a large mixing bowl until well combined. Using a wooden spoon stir in flour. Dough will be stiff.

Lightly flour a hard surface. Place dough on surface. Knead dough for about 5 minutes. Dough will become crumbly during the kneading process. Pull together and form dough into a ball.

Mix 1/2 cup of the sugar and 1/2 teaspoon of the cinnamon together in a small mixing bowl.

Take a generous tablespoon of dough and shape into ovals about 1/4 to 1/2 inch thick. Continue shaping cookies until dough is used. Dredge all the dough ovals in cinnamon-sugar mixture, coating both sides well.

Place cookies about 1-inch apart on a cookie sheet, ungreased. Brush very lightly with the beaten egg whites. Top with almonds and press in to stick to cookies.

Bake until edges are just firm and cookies are lightly browned. This should take about 9 to 11 minutes. Cool on wire racks.

Using two forks or tongs, dip cooled cookies into the Spiced Honey Glaze. Coat well. Let excess drip off as cookies are removed from the glaze. Place cookies on a sheet of parchment paper to set up about 30 minutes.

Spiced Honey Glaze

Ingredients

1/3 cup sugar

1/3 cup water

1/3 cup honey

1 tsp lemon zest

1 tbsp fresh lemon juice

1 cinnamon stick

1 whole clove

Directions

Combine all ingredients in a small saucepan. Stirring constantly, bring mixture to a boil. Boil until sugar is dissolved. Reduce heat to medium low. Simmer, uncovered, for 10 minutes. Remove from heat. Remove clove and cinnamon stick and discard.

Cool completely.

Notes

Made in the USA
San Bernardino, CA
29 September 2016